THE CHASE

Our Passionate Pursuit of Life Worth Living

DR. KIRK LEWIS

The Chase
Our Passionate Pursuit of Life Worth Living
by Dr. Kirk Lewis

Printed in the United States of America.

ISBN 9781498437509

Unless otherwise indicated, Bible quotations are taken from the New International Study Bible. Copyright © 1985 by The Zondervan Corporation.

www.xulonpress.com

ENDORSEMENTS

"Do not read this book unless you want to laugh, weep, think, and consider what the author reveals to the reader—an honest look at what it takes to walk with the Living, Loving Lord…complete with all the questions, confusions and ultimate confessions. Kirk Lewis, like his previous book, *Put Away Childish Things,* provides a way for both believers and non-believers to walk beside the men and women who walked beside Jesus. Lewis leads readers into this opportunity to consider what very easily could be the thoughts and actions of these real people as they encountered the Man from Nazareth.

"It will not take long to read this book. The words are not complicated. The chapters are not long. The stories may even be familiar if one has some knowledge of Scripture. However, you will need to take the time to see yourself in the pages. While Lewis' style is not formal, his message runs deep. I promise it is worth the trip!
I recommend *The Chase* only if you want to be changed—just like the people in the first century were changed when they walked with Jesus. Maybe, just maybe, their stories are our stories."

Dr. Grear Howard
Adjunct Faculty for Youth, Student and Family Ministry
Truett Seminary/Baylor University

"We seek to understand the Scripture through careful interpretation and through creative imagination. In this book Dr. Lewis demonstrates again his imaginative and poetic ability to help the Gospel stories come alive for us. He helps us to see old stories through a new lens. I commend his book to you."

Dr. Ron Lyles, Pastor
South Main Baptist Church, Pasadena, Texas,
and frequent contributing writer to BaptistWay Press

Other books and writings by Dr. Kirk Lewis

Put Away Childish Things
Published 2013 by Xulon Press

The Searcher
A Blog
www.drkirklewis.com

FORETHOUGHT

I love the Bible: the message it conveys, the truth it shares. I also love that it almost begs us to think and not to just accept things at face value. Even a cursory reading of Scripture reveals life-altering truth. So much more can be gained by studying God's Word more thoroughly—mining the rich ore of insight and wisdom that lies beneath the surface.

I readily admit that I'm not a Biblical scholar. I am, however, a student of Scripture. I love to learn the lessons God shares with me as I have read and reread the same Scriptures that I have studied most of my life. Depending on my circumstances, I typically find a new message or a new meaning for God's purpose and plan for my life every time I open the Bible. It is this process of spiritual growth and maturity that I crave as I chase after the heart of God.

Scripture tells us that if God's inspired writers tried to write down every good work Jesus did or every good word He uttered, the earth itself would be an insufficient library to contain the writings. That tells me that all those wonderful stories I heard as a child were highlights and snippets of much deeper conversations and a much broader message.

Before you read each story, let me encourage you to read the biblical reference provided. Where applicable, read the account of the story from each gospel. Many times the different writer added a piece of new information. Weave the stories together in your heart and head. I'm not trying to change the intent of God's Word, instead I encourage you to free your thoughts and look at these stories in a new way. I pray you find enough nuggets of God's gold to refresh your heart, inspire a closer walk with your Savior, and make you spiritually rich beyond your dreams.

ACKNOWLEDGEMENTS

After the words flow the first time,
no one knows with certainty
that there will be another story to tell.
Another book to write.

So much depends on
reader response.
Whether the message fell on
receptive ears.
Whether God opens new doors of opportunity.

My heart is grateful for the many readers of my first effort,
Put Away Childish Things,
who asked for more.

Your constant encouragement pushed me to begin again
despite a hectic schedule.
To open God's word.
Search its buried truths.
Commit those personal revelations to paper.

Thank you for helping me chase after a
richer and deeper
walk with Christ.

Without the encouragement of my readers,
the constant support of my
family and friends,
I'd still be dreaming.

DEDICATION

To my wife,
Robin.

Love beyond
Description.

Friendship for the
Decades.

Support for my
Dreams.

TABLE OF CONTENTS

Craving the Chase 15
Our Passionate Pursuit of Life Worth Living

The Discomforting Cost of Discipleship 23
The Rich, Young Ruler and the
Chase Ending in Missed Opportunity

Out on a Limb 35
Zacchaeus and the
Chase for Belonging

No Storm Too Great 49
The Tempest and the
Chase for Peace

Enter His Gates 61
The Cleansing of the Temple and the
Chase for Prayerful Worship

Making it Personnel 72
Nicodemus and the
Chase for a New Start

Thirsty No More 83
The Woman at the Well and the
Chase for Personal Revival

Gratitude of the Heart 96
The Thankful Leper and the
Chase for Genuine Gratitude

To See Things More Clearly 110
The Blind Man of Bethsaida and the
Chase for Discernment

Tale of Two Hearts 119
Martha Anointing Jesus and the
Chase for Mary's Heart

CRAVING THE CHASE

"Chase me, Grandpa!"
With a scream and a giggle,
he's off.

My four-year-old grandson Eli runs throughout our house,
both eyes twisted behind him in my direction,
heedless to what lies in front of him,
whether it's wall,
cabinet,
or little brother, Josiah.
He looks back…
To be certain I complied.
To find out how close I am.
His challenge dangles the carrot of
hugs as my reward.

When Eli calls,
I have a choice…

Procrastinate
Or
Pursue.

Though tired at times,
I yearn to bask in the glow of his love,
so I give it a merry chase replete with…
Shouts.
Screams.
Snickers.

Pure.
Unadulterated.
Joy.

When I catch him…
and he always lets me catch him…
we both get the hug we crave.
Falling to the floor in
complete contentment.
Resting in a twisted tangle
of arms and legs…
a hug of
divine delight.

That all-too brief moment of a grandfather's bliss
ends as he squirms from my grasp.
Running off again with
charmingly childish glee.
Once safely away,
he turns back with
a delightfully devilish grin,
throwing down a new challenge…

"Chase me again, Grandpa!
We're not finished!"

Though I think I could catch him anytime I want
the game would lose its luster if I…
caught him
too easily
or
quit
too early.

The thrill for both of us is found in
the chase.

*

Does this simple vignette of life
offer insight into our relationship with the Father?
I think it may.

When I committed my life to Christ,
God unleashed a chuckle for the ages,
rejoicing in the
restored relationship of
Creator
and
Created.

Oblivious, it seems, to the rest of the world,
He takes off running ahead of me...
"Chase me, Child!"
With screams, shouts, and snickers,
He's off!

Now, I have a choice.
Procrastinate
or Pursue.

Though tired at times,
I want to bask in the warmth of His love,
so I give Him a merry chase.
Pursuing with jubilation
the dangling carrots of
life abundant...
deep and dear
spiritual lessons for a life of
vast eternal value.

When I finally catch Him...
and He always lets me catch Him...
God and His child
share a moment of
complete contentment.
Resting in a twisted tangle
of arms and legs...
a hug of
Divine delight.

You see,
God could…
give me immediately
all I need to know and understand.

Transform me instantly
into everything He wants me to become.

Lay before me intentionally
every answer to every question
before I even know to ask.

Where is the gratification in that?
Where is the treasure in having life's answers
presented on a silver platter?

God made it so simple to receive His gift.
Accept Christ!
It's a snap.
Repent of my sin.
Seek forgiveness.
Believe in Him.
So simple it fits tightly in a tract.

Celebrate that salvation is…
A specific point in time.
A miraculous moment of faith.
Needed.
Necessary.

It's a good thing!

However,
experiencing His gift in its fullest remains far from simple.
Live for Christ!
That's the challenge.
Uncover the Truth.
Discover where I belong.
Recover from failed efforts.

Set aside the platitudes of the tract.
Celebrate that salvation is also...

A continuous process over time.
A series of maturing moments of faith.
Satisfying.
Sustaining.

Different
for each of us.

Dependent
on our unique call.

Determined
by our individual circumstance.

That's a good thing!

The thrill comes in the chase!
In running
after the heart of God.

In unearthing
the buried treasure that is
His will for my life.

In celebrating
with childlike wonder that the Creator God
wants me in that chase.

The good news...
I do not hopelessly pursue
someone who doesn't want to get caught.
God the Father sent His Son
to make it easier for us to catch Him.

The Bible stories in the New Testament I heard as a child
carried a simple message.
Truth of the salvation offered through Christ.

Truth of the faithful life
He called me to live.

At some point,
I quit the chase.
Content to accept the adolescent message.
Unwilling to pursue the adult meaning.

No more.
I found I could scarcely relate to the
choices they made, the
chances they took
because the lessons I learned as a child failed to
satisfy within the complex realities of my life.

Studying these stories again as an adult,
I find buried in the words left unsaid…
lost in the untold conversations…
a complex truth far more challenging
than I could ever imagined.

God demands more of me as an adult
than just believing.
Desires more of me than
punching a ticket to heaven.
God challenges me to chase after that which
makes me useful in
His Kingdom.

When I read the story of Zacchaeus,
I see more than a "wee little man" in a tree,
looking for a chance to see the miracle worker pass by.
I see a hurting soul
yearning for
purpose and belonging.

When Jesus cleared the Temple,
it was less about the moneychangers and
more about the need for authentic worship.
More about the obstacles put in the way of those
who genuinely seek God's presence.

He gave each of us the
chance to chase after His heart...
just as He did for those beloved characters
in the New Testament.

One of these characters never
caught what he was chasing.

The rich, young ruler,
ran headlong down the road in pursuit of Jesus
with a burning question on the tip of his tongue.
"What must I do..."
Sensing the magnitude of the
demand of discipleship,
he abandoned his chase.

The individuals who stuck it out,
those who engaged with Christ in honest dialogue,
hearts open to the possibilities,
always found that which they sought.

When they did...
after a moment of sheer bliss...
and unadulterated joy,
I just know Christ jumped to his feet,
pointed down the road
with a smile that lit the heavens...

"Chase me again, Child!"
We're not finished!"

The truth is...
we never finish our pursuit of all that God offers.
There is always more...
More to learn.
More to understand.
More to apply.

That's the lesson I've learned.
When I chase after God

21

in genuine quest for His will,
discovery always…
Leads to another question.
Opens another door.
Reveals more of the character of God.
Leaves me
craving the chase
for new truth.

If I pursue Him faithfully,
if I chase after His heart with mine,
the journey always ends the same…
God's arms wrapped around me.
Giggling in delight.
Squirming from my grasp.
Looking deeply into my heart.
Challenging me with the promise of
so much more.

"Chase me again, Child!"
We're not finished!"

Thanks to God!
It is a merry chase!

THE DISCOMFORTING COST OF DISCIPLESHIP
The Story of the Rich, Young Ruler
Matthew 19:16-30

"Wait, please!
Wait!"
Andrew heard the shouted plea.
Looked back down the road,
scanning the small crowd that followed Jesus.
A man waved wildly.
Running.
Swerving through the people.
Pausing long enough to help an elderly woman
pick up the bag of figs he accidentally knocked from her hands.
Resumed his sprint.
His colorful robe pulled up above his knees.
Hem clutched in his left hand.
"Please! Wait for me!"

Andrew,
always on the lookout for those seeking Jesus,
whistled to his companions ahead.
Jesus stopped.
Gazed over His left shoulder.
Saw the man running.
Jesus cocked his head inquisitively to the side.
Smiled at the rather comical sight.

Neriah.
Slightly rotund,
Robe billowing as he wove quickly through the crowd.
Head dress sliding slightly off the

right side of his head.
Sandals flopping,
kicking up dust from the well-travelled road.
The ungainly gait of the nonathletic.

When Neriah reached Jesus,
he fell to his knees at the Teacher's feet.
Part deference.
Part exhaustion.
Nodded in appreciation as Andrew gave him
a quick drink that allowed him time to breath and
gather his thoughts.

Jesus watched with a keen eye
as the man's gasping slowed to normal.
Sized him up.
No more than 20-years-old.
Obviously wealthy.
The cut of his clothes
betrayed his status.
Soft hands told Jesus they had never
wielded a mallet nor
wrestled a net.

After a moment,
Jesus helped the man to his feet.
Pointed his thumb casually down the road
in the direction they were heading before they stopped.
"You're welcome to join us," Jesus said.
"What is your name, and
what brings you here in such a hurry?"

"I am Neriah."
He spoke with a sense of urgency,
words flowing as a raging river.
Sharing his life story of...
Privilege.
Position.
Power.

A mother...
died while giving birth to a younger sister.

A father…
successful trader with
Cypress and Greece.
Lost at sea two years ago.
The family business now his inheritance.
Though young,
his great wealth
supported his standing in the community.
The pride he felt in his triumphs
mixed with a
tinge of loneliness.

The rich, young ruler stared into Jesus' eyes.
"Good Teacher,
I possess everything I need or want.
I'm restless.
Unsettled.
Can't sleep.
I've come to talk with you."

"Why have you come to me?"

Silent for a moment.
Neriah looked away,
finding it difficult to look Jesus in the eyes.
"I'm not sure.
There is something about you…"

For the next hour,
they talked.

Neriah recalled all he had seen and
heard over the past few weeks.
He had followed Jesus as he passed through the region.
Always near the back of the crowd.
Heard him challenge the Pharisees.
Pondered his insightful parables.
Saw him heal the deaf and lame.
Watched as he blessed the children in his arms.

Neriah smiled as he recalled the image of the
children crawling all over Jesus.

Tugged at the grass at his feet.
"I have a little boy at home.
Light of my life.
Love knows no depths.
Nothing I would not do for him."

I heard you say,
"Do not hinder them,
for the Kingdom of Heaven belongs to such as these."

As he repeated Jesus' words,
Neriah felt the same stirring in his heart
as he felt the night before.
"This is what I want.
What I want for my son."

Jesus saw the inner conflict.
Sat quietly.
Praying for the next question until…
It came.

"I know you are from God.
Good Teacher,
what good thing must I do to have eternal life?"

Jesus looked at him closely.
Serious intent.
Straightforward interest.
Sincere inquiry.

Saw a man awash with doubt.
Caught in the emotional eddy
of one too many miracles.
Swept away by the impassioned stirring
of one too many sermons.
Infatuated with the thought of Jesus, the Teacher,
Too willing to be one of his "students."
A Plato to his Socrates.

Jesus sought to temper the man's emotion.
Being caught up in the chase
is not the same as commitment.

"Why call me 'good'?
No one is good—except God."

Telling him, in essence,
"Look beyond the personality.
Calling me 'good,'
limits your understanding.
Set aside emotional enthusiasm.
Count the cost."

Jesus led a discussion concerning the law.
Do not murder.
Do not steal.
Do not.
Do not.
Do not.

Neriah felt his heart race.
Thought quickly through that which
he embraced all his life.
The moral code by which he faithfully lived.
The ethical behavior that
governed his business relationships.

"I have kept these commandments since a child.
I never...
would never...
harm anyone in these ways."

Warmed by his earnestness,
Jesus opened his heart to the young man.
Desired him to take the next necessary step.

He took Neriah by the elbow.
Guided him away from the road
toward a nearby field.
To look him in the eye without distraction.
They sat for a moment in silence on a stone wall
under the shade of a gnarled tree.

The Spirit
working in the rich man's heart
brought him to the
edge of an eternal choice.
The next step required a leap of faith.

Neriah sensed a
change in the conversation.
Heavy with gravity.
Thick with anticipation.

"You see those men?"
Jesus pointed to Peter and Andrew
sitting on the grass nearby.
Neriah studied the two brothers.
Acknowledged Jesus' question with a
imperceptible nod.
"They gave up everything to follow me.
Left home, family, and business
to walk the path I walk."

Jesus looked intently at the rich, young man.
They locked eyes.
"Can you do the same?"

Neriah's world
stopped spinning.
His mouth dropped open.
Puzzled by the implication of the question.

"Surely, you're not serious..."
his voice trailing away in confusion.
For the first time
uncomfortable in the company of the Teacher.

Sensing a critical juncture in their conversation,
Jesus spoke softly.
"Listen carefully to what I'm saying."

"You do so much that is right and good,
but I sense..."
Jesus paused in mid-sentence,

looking down at his calloused hands.
Not a command He gave lightly.

"You lack one thing…"
Then, he looked up at the young man,
willing him to respond with an open heart.

"Go, sell all you have.
Give it to the poor.
Do this and your treasure will be great in heaven.
Once you do this,
come back and
follow me."

Stunned disbelief.
Deafening silence.
The internal struggle of a young man's heart.
Eyes darted in every direction,
as if deciding which direction to run.
Mouth opened and closed several times,
like a fish flopping on a beach,
gasping for a breath of water.

He stood.
Turned away from Jesus.
Deep in thought,
Lost in internal debate.
Rested his arms on a low-hanging branch.
Chin upon his fist.

From the day he was born,
he never wanted for anything.
His house.
His servants.
His business.
His wealth.
All a source of family pride.
An inheritance from a father he adored.
He could not imagine a life lived as a
destitute disciple.
Wandering from village to village,
Surviving on the hospitality of strangers.

He turned pleadingly to Jesus.
Took Him by the hand.
His eyes said it all.
"You can't ask me to do this.
It's too much!"

Jesus peered into Neriah's soul,
imploring him to understand the commitment required.
Standing on the brink of eternity,
the rich, young ruler...
blinked.

Face fell.
Shoulders slumped.
Sadness gripped his soul.
He pulled his hand from the Savior's grasp.
Turned away.
Walked wearily home.

The man who lacked nothing,
left lacking everything.

The Chase Ending in Missed Opportunity

Three gospel writers
captured this most tragic story.
Seared in memory.
Sealed for eternity.

The rich, young ruler.
By virtue of wealth and position...
Distinctive
among men.
By family heritage and religious code...
Devoted
to moral living.
By personal choice and business practice...
Dedicated
to unquestioned ethics.
By the emptiness of his soul and conviction of the Spirit...

Declared himself a
genuine seeker of truth.

He raced to the feet of Christ
harboring an honest desire to follow Him.
He left the shadow of grace
rejecting a tough lesson about the
cost of discipleship.

"What good thing must I do to receive eternal life?"

A question of longing and emptiness.
Neriah lived obediently by the commandments.
Acknowledged with some degree of pride,
"I've kept them all."
Never murdered.
Never stolen.
Never committed adultery.
Never harmed another soul.
Have never.
Would never.

Lived by the letter of the law.
Languished in the onerous weight of orthodoxy.
Emptiness left a gaping
hole in his heart.
Misguided obedience to a set of rules
strangled all joy.
So, he set aside dignity and
ran after Jesus.

Jesus believed him.
Saw the sincerity of soul.
Recognized good character.
Scripture tells us Jesus loved him for it.
Here was a man who
had all he needed and more.
Had amassed through inheritance and hard work
a wealth to be envied.
On this day,

31

he knelt in deep respect at the feet of the Teacher,
looking for the missing piece of life's puzzle.

Jesus' challenge was simple.
Cease seeing "goodness" as the end-all answer.
Cease seeing "goodness" as
a matter of not doing bad things.
So, you've not hurt anyone.
Great!
Your piety allows you to thank God
that you are not like the
sinners and tax collectors.
What an uninspiring way to live!

Jesus threw down an unexpected gauntlet.
Think less upon the laws not broken.
More about the broken lives about which you've
thought nothing.

Take that with which you have been blessed.
Give it to those in need.
Use God-given gifts…
Relieve suffering of the sick.
Ease misery of the wounded.
Lift up the mistreated.
Encourage the hopeless.

Be the hands of God in a hurting world.

Jesus drew the man away from all that was comfortable
to live the gloriously
discomforting adventure of discipleship.
For all his noble living,
this he could not do.

The wealthy man chose poorly.
The man who lacked nothing,
lacked everything.
Turned away at his most
personal turning point.

Sad reality in a troubled world...
good men and women still stand at the
edge of eternity.
Discovering that goodness...
for the sake of goodness...
leaves a burning hole in the soul.

Good men and women
come to Jesus with intense
desire to discover
what they must do to find
purpose and fulfillment.
Seeking the one act of goodness that finally releases
Heaven's blessings.
When the demand seems too great,
asks too much,
they turn from the welcoming eyes of the Father.
Selfish hearts.
Slumped shoulders.
Sad souls.
Choosing to consider
discipleship a hardship...
rather than a blessing.

Goodness will never substitute for grace.

Bonus lesson for believers.

The tragedy of the ruler forces me
to reassess my
personal priorities.
To reaffirm that
"goodness" does not equal "godliness."

The rich, young ruler reminds me...
avoid spiritual complacency that convinces me that
"good" is good enough...
complacency that no longer yearns to be
more like Christ each day.

Christ says to me,
"Rid yourself of the
complacency caused by compliance
to a list of
do's or don'ts."

Instead, He calls me as He called the rich, young ruler.
Set aside...
Things I cherish.
Things I refuse to yield.
Things I place as priority.
Things I build as barricades to keep God away.

Step outside my comfort zone, and
with all that is within me...

Chase after the gloriously
discomforting
adventure of
discipleship.

The rich, young ruler missed his chance.
I dare not waste the opportunities
God gives me
to be uncomfortable in my own walk of faith.

"Search me, God and know my heart;
test me and know my anxious thoughts.
See if there is any offensive way within me,
and lead me in the way of understanding."
Psalm 139:23-24

OUT ON A LIMB
The Story of Zacchaeus
Luke 19:1-9

The small band of travelers
ambled down the eastern bank of the Jordan River.
Spread out over a short distance.
Clustered in small groups of
two or three.
Occupied in casual conversation.
Good friends.
Talking about
everything and nothing.

Jesus.
Walked alone.
Near the river bank.
Occasionally picking up a small, flat stone.
Skipping it across the river.

Matthew.
Walked alone.
Trailing the pack by a good distance.
Lost in contemplation.
Troubled by the incident with the rich man
two days earlier.

The rich, young ruler had raced after the Master Teacher,
seeking a clearer understanding of the things
he must do to receive eternal life.
Eager.

Excited.
Expectant.

Matthew recalled the conversation
in snippets.

"Obey the law,"
Jesus said.

"I've done it,"
the man replied.

Looking into his heart, Jesus cut to the chase.
"Sell everything.
Then, give it away."

Matthew remembered the look in the rich man's eyes
as he turned away.
The man who had everything,
walked away with nothing.
Remembered just as clearly the sadness in Jesus' eyes.

"It is easier for a camel to pass through the
eye of a needle
than for a rich man to enter the
kingdom of God."

A tough word of warning.
Especially for the former tax collector.
Once, he lived
a life of abundance.
Now, he lived
an abundant life.
There was a significant difference.
Amid his personal reflection,
Matthew found himself thinking
about a friend.

He quickened his pace.
Caught up to his Master.
Walked in silence for a moment beside him.

Picking up stones.
Skipping them on the water like Jesus.
Each trying to get more hops than the other
amid some good-natured teasing.

After a time,
Matthew turned to Jesus.

"I have a favor to ask."

Jesus looked at him curiously.
Matthew never asked for anything.

"Certainly.
What can I do for you today?"

"I have this friend…
in Jericho."

*

He walked the streets of Jericho.
Stepping lightly from door to door.
Lagging far enough behind the scurrying crowd to be…
Inconspicuous.
Ignored.

He carried a chip on his shoulder.
Bitterness in his spirit.
Loneliness in his soul.

Undersized.
Unimposing.
Adorned with the trappings of wealth
earned as the region's
Chief Tax Collector.
Resented for it.

Zacchaeus.
Detested
by his neighbors.

37

Despised
as a Roman collaborator.
Denied
any sense of belonging.

He followed a massive crowd
gathering at the gates of Jericho.
Word spread quickly.
Jesus,
the Teacher.
Crossed the Jordan
heading to Jerusalem.
On the outskirts of Jericho.

Pariah among the people.
Few talked directly to Zacchaeus...
Except to curse his...
birth,
bearing, and
being.

But Zacchaeus listened.
He always listened.
Overheard their stories.
Pretended not to hear as they spoke of Jesus'
ministry and
miracles.

Grew curious as they called him a friend of the...
Ordinary.
Outsiders.
Outcasts.

Zacchaeus had to see for himself.

*

Daunting surge
of the crowd.
Deafening sound
of cheers.

Again.
And over again.
Zacchaeus found a spot at the edge of the road
Just to be brushed aside.
Elbowed out of the way.

Regarded with
contempt.

Treated with
condescension.

Viewed as little more
than a caricature
unworthy of consideration.

He found himself…
Pushed.
Provoked.
Peppered with insults.

Zacchaeus could not see over.
Could not push through.
He would miss his chance
to see Jesus.

Caught in the ebb and flow,
Zacchaeus stumbled against a tree.
Grabbed a thick branch to keep from falling.
Protected by its trunk.
Catching his breath.
Zacchaeus stared at the low branches and saw a
perfect perch
to see the
passing processional.

He climbed nimbly onto a limb hanging over the roadway.
Seven feet above the ground.
Beyond the reach of the
unruly crowd.
Zacchaeus waited.

Jesus and his disciples rounded the corner.
Surrounded by a throng of people.

Singing
adoration.

Shouting
approval.

Zacchaeus watched from his roost.
Jesus stopped several times along the way...
Spoke a private word
To an invalid woman.
Scooped a four-year-old boy into his arms,
laughed as he tousled his hair.
Love and kindness
apparent in his smile.
A personal touch for everyone.

Zacchaeus brushed away the moisture building in his eyes
with the sleeve of his robe.
So long since
anyone smiled at him that way.
At that moment,
he had never felt more alone.
The constant hatred he endured
suddenly overwhelming.

As Jesus walked slowly his direction,
Zacchaeus' mind drifted back.
It had not always been this way.

He took his post as chief tax collector
with an honest heart.
Sincere spirit.

Others abused the position.
Exorbitant rates.
Far beyond the requirement of Rome.
Zacchaeus wanted
desperately to be different.
To ease the burden on his neighbors.

Scorned
for his trouble.
Spurned
despite his effort.

Even though no one paid more than he owed,
they never saw it that way.
Never saw him that way.

Zacchaeus sighed.
To think this man walking down the street
might be different...
Pipe dreams.
Wishful thinking.
Beyond hope.

The little man in the tree woke from his daydream.
Startled by the roar of the crowd.

From where he sat,
Zacchaeus blinked his eyes.
Not believing who he saw walking next to Jesus,
constantly scanning the crowd
as if looking for someone.

Matthew.
Tax collector from Galilee.
Colleague from his past.
What was he doing with this man?

Matthew looked vaguely his direction.
Leaned into Jesus.
Whispered in his ear.

Pointed down the road.
Jesus grinned.
Nodded.
Continued down the street.
Toward the tree.
Toward Zacchaeus.

Jesus stopped under the tree,
enjoying the cool shade.
Zacchaeus could not bring himself to shout out.
Sat silently in the sycamore.

The man glanced up through the drooping leaves.
Strained to see into the shadows.
Zacchaeus moved behind the trunk.
Fearful of drawing the attention of the crowd.
Afraid of being mocked as a fool.

A hand pushed aside the lower branches beneath Zacchaeus.
At that moment,
the tax collector and the Teacher
looked into each other's eyes.
A grin as warm as the sun greeted Zacchaeus.

"Well, hello there."
Jesus chuckled quietly.
"You must be Zacchaeus.
Matthew told me all about you.
Why don't you come down now?"
More request than command.

Zacchaeus hesitated only a moment.
Jumped from the tree.
Landed lightly at Jesus' feet.

Zacchaeus was swept off his feet in a bear hug.
Matthew embraced Zacchaeus
as friends lost to each other for years.
Matthew spun him around.
Introduced him to Jesus.

Jesus and Zacchaeus shook hands.
Spoke quietly for a minute.

A hush fell over the shocked crowd.
Stunned silence spoke
volumes about the
hatred in their hearts.

Jesus frowned at the crowd.
His eyes narrowed.
Then, he looked down at Zacchaeus.
Slapped him on the back.
Laughed a hearty laugh.

"Take me to your house, please.
I'm feeling a bit hungry."

Leaving a muttering and mumbling crowd behind,
the Teacher and the tax collector
took salvation's first steps.

*

Jesus and Zacchaeus spent the day…
Reclining at the table.
Sharing a meal.
Swapping stories.
Zacchaeus shared his heart about his work.
His desire to do right by his people.

Jesus nodded knowingly.
Understanding completely what it's like to be
rejected by those too blind to see the truth.

"We have that in common."

With those words,
Jesus shared His purpose.
The Messiah.
Sent to seek and save those who are lost…

Separated from God…
Bound by ritual and routine.

Toward the end of the day,
Zacchaeus and Jesus
walked to the door of his home.
Looked at the gawkers standing outside,
so agitated that Jesus spent time in the
presence of the publican.

Zacchaeus turned to Jesus.
"I thought I was living as God wanted me to live.
This loneliness is too much to bear.
Riches never enough to satisfy.
I want to taste what you offer…"

"Today,
My life is yours.
You are my Lord."

In response to grace,
Zacchaeus promised a changed life…

"Half of all I possess to the poor…"
"If I cheated anyone,
I'll repay four times as much."

Jesus stared intently into the
eyes of the tax collector.
Reading his soul.

"Salvation has come to this house."

He embraced Zacchaeus.
"…a true Son of Abraham."

*

That next day,
Jesus and his disciples waved farewell to Zacchaeus.
Continuing their journey to Jerusalem.

Jesus walked with Matthew.
Side by side in silence.
Lost in thought about the
small man with a big heart.

After a few miles and
without warning,
Jesus threw an arm around his disciple.
Wrestled him into an affectionate headlock.
Spun him around twice
like a whirlwind.
Pushed him playfully away.
Grinning from ear to ear.

"Think about it, Matthew,"
Jesus twirled in a complete circle,
arms outstretched as if embracing the world.
He locked eyes with this tax collector turned disciple.

"Somewhere, my wonderful friend,
a camel just passed through the eye of needle."

Jesus danced in the middle of a dusty road.
Joy amid his journey
to the cross.

The Chase for Belonging

A rich and respected ruler
ran a great distance in his quest for eternal life.
In the end,
he rejected the
righteousness God required.

Zacchaeus,
a rich and reviled man,

shunned by an angry crowd,
climbed out on a limb in a quest for meaning
not found in his
work or his wealth.
In the end,
he embraced the encounter with Christ and
gloried in the grace of God.

What was so different about the two men?

Both ran after Jesus.
One knowing exactly what he wanted.
The other knowing exactly what he needed.
One unwilling to let go of what he had.
The other willing to embrace what he could become.

We want Jesus to be clairvoyant.
To know the needs of strangers who cross His path.
To get a sixth sense that someone in need
sits secretly out of sight in a stately Sycamore.

Could it be that Matthew,
a tax collector whose life had changed through his
walk with the Savior,
laid the groundwork for a divine encounter between the
tax collector and the Teacher?

It is a story of...
Grace extended.
Grace considered.
Grace received.
Those of us seeking to live a life of faith
find great beauty in its telling...
on so many levels.

I need to be
Zacchaeus...
Wanting so badly to encounter Christ
because life has left me lonely.
Willing to go out on a limb to catch a simple glimpse of Him

because to be in His presence brings comfort.
Wishing, beyond hope, to be embraced by Him,
because I feel so disconnected.

Responding to his voice as he beckons me
because His words convict and compel me to change.
Spending time in deep conversation
because I need to hear Him declare that I am a
"true child of Abraham."

Maybe I am Zacchaeus…
sometimes.

I want to be
Matthew…
Convicted of a friend's need for Jesus
because I want him to share my sense of
purpose and peace.
Willing to take his name to Christ
because I know He is the only Way
provided by Scripture.
Praying for an opportunity to bring them together.
Introducing him to my Savior.
Dancing in the dusty street in sheer delight that my
friend's encounter with Christ
changed the direction of his life.

Maybe I am Matthew…
sometimes.

Far too often, I am
the crowd.
Cheering for Jesus on His journey to Jerusalem
to take up His cross in my stead.
Singing praises.
Shouting in adoration.
Standing in the way of the little guy
trying to catch a glimpse of the Savior.
Elbowing him out of my way.
Finding every reason to push him away.

To discredit him.
To disparage him.
To disengage from one whom
I deem a sinner.
Somehow less deserving of God's touch.
Murmuring in discontent when Jesus
calls him from the tree…
blesses his life
instead of mine.

In this I am reminded…
the critic of sinners cannot be a
witness to sinners.

My prayer.
"Lord.
Take away the sense of superiority that
so often places me in the crowd.
Create in me the…
Heart of Matthew.
Spirit of Zacchaeus."

"For the Lord is a sun and shield;
the Lord bestows favor and honor:
No good thing does He withhold from
those whose walk is blameless.
Lord Almighty,
blessed is the one who trusts in you."
Psalm 84:11-12

NO STORM TOO GREAT

The Story of the of the Tempest
Mark 4:35-41

The small oil lamps flickered,
casting eerie shadows on the wall.
A small group of men reclined around the dinner table
in a small home
in a small village
just beyond the walls of Jerusalem.

The men engaged in relaxed conversation.
Reverent.
Respectful.
Paid tribute to their guest.

Simon.
The Zealot.
Devoted disciple.
Willing witness
to the power of the risen Lord.

Older now.
Deep lines of age and experience
etched in a weathered face.
Hair and beard
liberally sprinkled with strands of gray.
Eyes still danced with life
as he talked of his Master.
Awe filled his voice as he told story after story
of his life with his Lord.

A young missionary sat among those gathered in the room.
Eagerly recorded the aging disciple's stories.
Probed his elder with
question upon question.
John Mark.
Younger brother in Christ.
Wanted to learn as much as he could
from one who walked with Jesus.

"Tell me more."

Simon closed his eyes.
Breathed deeply.
Looked back in time to the...
Infinite conversations.
Incredible experiences.
Indelible memories.

John Mark's question penetrated his musing.
"What do you remember most?"

Without opening his eyes,
Simon said,
"I remember the storm."

*

The young disciple walked along the
crest of a hill overlooking the Sea of Galilee.
One among a huge crowd.
Several thousand strong.
Gathered at this remote seaside location
searching for...
Harmony.
Healing.
Hope.

Simon smiled.
Looked midway down the slope.
One never had to search for Jesus.
Simply find the tightest knot of people.

Jesus would be standing in the middle.
The disciple found him among a cluster of families.
Men and women.
Boys and girls.

Always at work…
Easing suffering.
Extending blessings.
Expressing kindness.

Simon and the other disciples
ministered as they had been taught.
As he moved among the people,
Simon kept one eye on his Master.
Amazed at His patience.
Awed by His capacity to capture a moment.
Astonished by His ability to…
Tune out every distraction.
Care for the one before him
as if the two of them
stood alone on the mountainside and not
surrounded by a multitude.

Jesus made time for everyone.
A smile.
A hug.
A prayer.
A listening ear.
A gift of His divine presence.

The afternoon grew late.
Simon shuffled away from the crowd.
Walked down to the beach.
Crossed his arms.
Leaned against a boulder.
A long, but lovely day neared its end.
Waited for what he knew would come.

Ministry invariably led to a message.
Jesus cared for the physical needs of those He encountered.

Yet, He never left them without
spiritual nourishment and healing.
He would teach before sending the crowd home.

As often happened when his heart was at peace,
his body at rest,
Simon recalled the day Jesus asked him
to walk away from all he had known.
A memory as vivid this day
as it was so many months ago.

*

"Simon,"
Jesus said as he encountered the man
among a crowd of rebels.
"You've spent your life doing things to make you rich.
I know you aren't happy.
I see it in your eyes.
Follow me.
I'll show how amazing life can be
without all that hatred."

The former freedom fighter
shook his head in wonder.
Embarrassed slightly by the smile plastered on his face.
No tinge of disappointment with his decision.
Simon was blessed, and
he knew it.

*

Jesus called out to James and Peter,
shaking Simon from his private thoughts.
He looked up the hillside.
Spread above him, a field of
men, women, and children.
Ripe for the harvest.

52

After a quick word of instruction from Jesus,
James and Peter untethered their boats.
Jesus waved for the other disciples.

"Climb aboard.
I'll speak from the boat.
It will be easier for everyone to hear."

Simon.
Never comfortable on the water,
smiled a sheepish grin.
Turned a slight shade of green.
Settled himself wearily on the sand,
his sore back flat against the rock.
Patted the sandy soil.
"I'll be fine right here."

With a familiar, bemused expression Simon knew too well,
Jesus tossed his head back.
Laughed good-naturedly at the
disciple's discomfort.

"Have it your way,
my friend."

The men shoved the boat into the water.
Anchored 30 feet offshore.
Used the water as a
natural amplifier for His message.
Jesus sat in the prow of the boat.
Lifted His arms to quiet the murmuring crowd.

Simon listened with rapt attention.
Mesmerized by Jesus' words.
Parable after parable.
Truth after truth.
Pierced through the personal barriers
of those with ears to hear.

A sower.
A lamp.
A mustard seed.

Undiscovered
truth waiting to be
discovered.

An invitation to the impoverished
to experience God's kingdom.

A final prayer, and
the people drifted home.

Simon watched them leave.
Helped his friends gather the supplies
as Jesus visited with the stragglers.

After a time, and weary of the work,
Jesus called his disciples.
Stifled a yawn.
Twelve men yawned in sympathy.

"We need some time to ourselves.
Let's take the boats to the other side."

The sun disappeared in a gray haze
behind the hills of Galilee.
Night fell quickly.
Exhausted from the day,
Jesus laid down on a pillow near the rudder.
John quietly steered the ship slipping
silently along with the steady wind.

Simon sat in the middle of the boat.
Talked quietly with Thomas.
White knuckles gripped tightly on
the side of the hull.
Fearful of the open water.

A distant clap of thunder echoed over the water.
At first...
little more than a steady vibration,
reverberating on the skin.
Within minutes...
like a clash of cymbals and heavy roll of drums.
Sails rippled with the
first fresh gust of wind.
The tiny boat rocked on the gathering waves.

Simon glanced at John,
who spoke urgently to his brother, James.
The brothers shouted words to Andrew and Simon
piloting the second boat nearby.
Debated seriously whether to
turn back or
press forward.
Rain fell in sheets
before they could decide.

Fearsome winds.
Flashes of lightning.

Rolling thunder.
Roiling waves.

Battered boats.
Buffeted passengers.

Simon cried out in dread as
wave after wave
swamped the boat.
Clinging to the side with one hand.
Vainly bailing water from the hold with the other.
In the stern,
James and John screamed in defiance to the
wind and waves.
Fearlessly struggled against the elements.
Frightened by their lack of control.
A wave tossed the vessel deep into the trough,

spilling supplies overboard.
The disciples hung on in desperation.
Simon looked again to the stern…
where Jesus
slept serenely.

Simon soon found his voice.
Joining the other disciples in a chorus of screams
intended to wake Jesus from his slumber.
Simon crawled on his belly in the
bottom of the boat,
shaking Jesus by His shoulders.

"Master,
please, wake up!"

The disciple screamed in Jesus' ear,
trying to be heard against the raging storm.

"How can you sleep?
Do you not care if we drown?"

Jesus opened His eyes.
Blinked twice.
Quickly took in His surroundings.
Hearing the frightened cries of His closest friends.
Pulled himself to a standing position.
Gripped the helm with one hand.
Raised the other above His head.
Shouted to the
wind and waves.

"Be still!"

More quickly than it began,
the wind ceased to blow.
Sea grew flat.
Rain stopped.
Clouds parted.
Moon shone.

Perfect peace.
Complete calm.

The terror of the blackest night
yielded to the awe of God's might.

Simon.
Hair dripping wet.
Matted in strands plastered to his bearded cheeks.
Coughed up a little bitter water.
Gazed at the moonlight shining on
the placid waters of the
Sea of Galilee.
Stared in wonder
into the face of Jesus.

The Master stood at the helm,
Disappointed.
Disheartened.

"Why are you so afraid?"

His voice clearly heard in the stillness of the night,
carrying even to those in the nearby boat.

"Do you still have no faith?"

He moved quietly to the prow of the boat.
Touched each man on the shoulder as he passed.
Gentle rebuke.
Gentler reassurance.
Sat staring ahead toward the distant shore.
Lost in thought.

Simon.
Whispered in
utter astonishment.
Absolute admiration.

"Who is this that even the wind and waves obey him?"

*

In the quiet of evening, an older and wiser
Simon emerged from the haze of his memory.
Aware again of the presence of John Mark
and the others sitting around the table.
Spellbound.
Silent.

"We should have known,"
Simon said,
voice little more than a raspy whisper.
Tears filling his eyes.

Pointed to his chest.
"I should have known."

"No storm is too great."

Simon affectionately squeezed
John Mark's knee as he rose from the table.
Looked to every person in the room...

"Who is this that the wind and waves obey?"

"He is
Jesus Christ."

The Chase for Peace

I look in the mirror.
Find Simon staring back at me.

I find myself...
Sitting on the beach.
Leaning against a rock.
Basking in the glow of the Son.
Soaking up the sunshine of His wisdom.
Comfortable after a day of serving.

Just when I think it can't get any better,
God calls.

"Get in the boat."

I face another Spirit-led journey
outside my comfort zone.

I push off in this ship of
God's choosing.
A death grip on the hull as I float
further from the safety of my shore.

Then, the first squall hits.
"God, I *knew* this would happen.
I got in the boat like You asked.
Why the rough seas?"

Wind picks up.
Waves crash.
I cry out for the comfort of
beach and boulder.

On the verge of sinking into the swirling waters,
I finally turn to God,
certain He lies
asleep in the stern.
Unaware of my turmoil.

A prayer of desperation.
A plea for deliverance.

"Wake up, Lord.
Don't you know I'm drowning?"
Less question.
More demand.

Amid my terrified rant,
God grips the helm.
Tames the tempest
in my soul.

Then, I hear…

"Do you have so little faith?"

I am never promised clear sailing.
Storms happen.
I could stay on the beach,
but that's not always where He needs me.

Sometimes,
He needs me on the other side of the lake.
Sometimes,
that means passing through the storm.

If I must pass through the tempest to get there,
this is what I need to know...

My Savior is in the boat.
Comfortably in control.

If He sails with me,
the boat won't sink.
No matter how great the storm.
It's as simple as that.

Who is this that the wind and waves obey?

He is Jesus Christ.
My Savior.

*"The Lord is close to the brokenhearted and
saves those crushed in spirit.
The righteous may have many troubles,
but the Lord delivers him from them all."
Psalm 34:18-19*

ENTER HIS GATES
The Story of the Cleansing of the Temple
Mark 11:15-17

She shuffled inside the Temple through its eastern gate,
caught in a stream of
hurrying humanity.
Pressing.
Pushing.
Prodding.
An exhausting effort to
pass through the portal.

The massive crowd created an instant bottleneck
at the narrow opening.
Hundreds tried to enter
like sheep herded into a pen.

The petite, elderly woman.
Jostled.
Jolted.
Jammed through the doorway.
Once inside,
some hurried soul shoved her to the side.
Knocked her off balance,
scraping her wrist on the rough, stone wall.

She scanned the courtyard of the women,
rubbing the abrasion on her hand.
Blaring noise.
Braying animals.
Barked insults.

Smells and sounds stunned her senses.
Every face that passed reflected a patience worn thin
by long lines.
Angry haggling.
Inhospitable hearts.

Slowly, she meandered through the booths,
handing over her Temple tax.
Paying her pennies
for a sacrificial dove.
Exorbitant fees left two coins in her bag.

A Jewish convert from Syria.
A trip of a lifetime.
A demanding and dangerous
journey to Jerusalem.
In her heart,
Worth every toilsome step to pray
to the living God.
In His home.
His temple.

Pictured this moment in her heart for years, but
she never expected such...
unholiness
in this most Holy place.

Passed through the masses
deeper into the Court of the Gentiles,
seeking a quieter place to pray.
Hawkish vendors pawed at her arms,
Plying their wares.
When she did not buy,
They pushed her away.
Cursed her family.
Cruel words.
Contemptuous sneers.

She moved again.
Longing to feel God's presence in
His Temple.

Once...
Someone arguing with an elder of the Temple
broke her reverent conversation.

Twice...
Someone yelled at her
as she settled to her knees.

Three times...
Someone shoved her against the wall
as they jockeyed for position.

Tears flowed down her wrinkled face.
Tired.
Traumatized.

Disillusioned.
Disheartened.

*

A few minutes before,
Jesus and His disciples entered the Temple Court
through the same eastern gate.
A long journey from Capernaum
in obedience to the call of Passover.
The last Passover
before the passion
of the cross.

Jesus steeled himself against the revulsion He felt
Every time He entered the unruly atmosphere.
Particularly rowdy and quarrelsome this year.

Muttered to His disciples,
"How can anyone worship like this?"

Worked His way through the crowd,
brushing aside the moneychangers and sellers.
Hearing the relentless haggling over

price and
product.
Anger boiled with each passing moment.

Jesus' head snapped to a commotion on His left.
An elder in the Temple.
Shouted and shamed
a man who refused to pay the asking price for a
blemished lamb.
Unsuitable for sacrifice.
Unworthy of God's blessing.

Too late Jesus stepped to intervene.
The elder drove the man back
with fisted rebuke,
pushing him into and over an elderly woman
kneeling at the wall.
Offering her prayers amid the
Chaos.
Confusion.

The Master could tolerate no more.
Grabbed two cords from a vendor's stand.
Wrapped them around His wrist.
Held tightly in His calloused hand.
A crack of the improvised whip.
A shout that bounced off the Temple walls,
Jesus cried out,

"Enough!"

People spun around.
Stared.
Shocked.

The old woman backed against the wall.
Avoided the man in the dusty robe as He charged by.
She watched in awe as He…
Moved quickly to a moneychanger's table,
tossing it aside as if it were made of papyrus.

64

Scattered a bag full of coins
across the dusty ground.
Pushed over a nearby fence holding a small herd of sheep.
Drove them toward the gate and
outside the Temple.

People scattered.
Ran from the Man with furious eyes.

Above the din,
she heard again…

"Enough!"

Picking up an armful of cages holding the doves,
the Man shoved them forcefully
into the arms of a Temple guard.

"Take them and go!
Now!"

The elderly woman startled with fright.
A burly merchant jumped in front of the Man.
Beefy hands stretched out to stop Him.
Eyes intent on malice.

The Man with the whip froze.
Held the index finger of His right hand
inches from the merchant's face.
Dark eyes glared at the storekeeper.
An explicit,
unspoken
message.

"Don't even think about it!"

The merchant cowered.
Grabbed his possessions.
Fled toward the gate without looking back.

The woman stood with her mouth agape.
Fascinated by the
presence and power
on display.

As He encountered each Gentile worshipper,
He looked intently into their eyes.
Urged them,

"Please wait."

Then, in a whirlwind of God's wrath,
He would turn to another merchant,
driving them from the Temple.

A swirl of dust.
The Man stretched out his arms.
Grabbed the edge of the heavy wooden gates.
Watched the mass of fleeing humanity.

"My Father's house is for *all* nations a house of prayer.
You have turned it into a den of thieves!"

"Enough!"

Slammed shut the doors.
Sealed the ensuing silence
into the courtyard of God's Temple.

The elderly woman and dozens of desiring worshippers
Stood still.
Shaken.
Silent.

*

Jesus stood still at the entrance.
Breathing heavily.
Head bowed.
Tears of sadness stained dusty cheeks.

Rubbed His eyes and face
as He calmed His emotions.

Troubled worshippers…
Clung tightly to one another.
Clustered in tiny groups,
gathered across the courtyard.

Shocked priests…
Huddled in the far corner.
Trembling in a mixture of
terror and temper.

Stunned disciples…
Stood slack-jawed amid the overturned tables.
Astonished at the demonstration of physical power
never seen from their Lord.

Jesus looked at His closest friends.
Exhaled deeply.
Puffed out His reddened cheeks.
Shook His head slightly and…
with visible relief, winked.
"I'm okay."

Jesus scanned the silent assembly.
Looked intently for the elderly woman caught in the middle.
He found her.
Crouched in a corner.
Leaning against the wall.
Knees pulled tightly to her chest.

He sat down beside her.
Smiled a self-conscious grin.

"I'm sorry you had to see that,
but I know you came to worship our God."

He pushed himself upward,
pressing His back against the stone wall.

He took her hands.
Led her to the center of the courtyard,
calling for the others to join Him.
In the stillness of that moment,
Jesus led them in quiet prayer.

He motioned to the frightened priests.
Signaled them to quietly accept the offered sacrifices.
One by one.
The worshippers relinquished their tribute.
Moved to a quiet place.
Offering private praise
to the Lord Almighty.

Jesus watched the prayerful pass.
Spoke quiet words of encouragement.

The old, Syrian woman
moved slowly in the line of worshippers.
Waited for her moment to offer her dove to the priest.
As the line moved slowly forward, she
stopped in front of the Man who cleared the Temple.
With a look of gratitude,
raised a shaking hand,
placed it delicately on his cheek.
Patted it twice.
Inner joy burst forth in a near toothless smile,
erasing 20 years from her elderly features.

Laughing quietly,
Jesus offered His arm.
They shuffled to a quiet corner.
Knelt together in the dust.
Offered praise and worship to the Father.

The Chase for Prayerful Worship

What made this Passover different?

The same chaotic scene had played itself out
every year upon Jesus' arrival for Passover.
The crowds.
The clamor.
The irreverence.

Every time He came to the Temple,
He winced.
Overwhelmed by the
cacophony within the courtyard.
Sickened by the difficulty of
worship amid the clamor.

Yet,
He never reacted outwardly to His
inner revulsion...
never yielded to the rising bile of anger in His throat.

Different this time.
This time He would enter Jerusalem's Temple
for the last time...
on His way to the cross.

Jesus chose this time to make a bold statement
about worship.
Misunderstood by the myopic
Temple authorities.

In a graphic way...
Reminded them that God's house is a
place of reverence.

In a graphic way...
Confirmed that personal prayer lies at the
heart of worship.

In a graphic way...
Warned against attitudes and behaviors that
impede the worship of another.

In a graphic way...
Insisted that God's house would be an
inviting place of prayer...
for all nations.

For all people.

Imagine a church with...

No distractions.
No dissension.
No disdain for the different.

A church with...
No elitism.
No exclusivity.

A church with...
No arrogance.
No attitude that shuns the seeker.
No action that
serves as a stumbling block to
real worship.

Imagine a church with...
doors and hearts wide open.
Ready for worship.

A church for whom...
God's house echoes with prayer and praise...
for all people.

Just imagine.
Then...
Make it so.

"Enter his gates with Thanksgiving;
His courts with praise,
Give thanks to Him and
Praise His name."
Psalm 100:4

MAKING IT PERSONAL
The Story of Nicodemus
John 3:1-16

Eleven men lay a short distance from the fire.
Wishing for sleep after a long day.
Two others spoke quietly.
Laughed easily,
Careful to keep their voices low.
Warmed by
campfire
and
companionship.
Familiar as brothers.

Another,
face veiled by the hood of his cloak,
tiptoed at the edge of darkness.
Hidden in the shadows of the night.
Slowly circling the campfire.
Gathering courage.

Watched.
Waited.

The men gathered near the light
were an enigma to the
man in the dark.
Uneducated.
Unremarkable.
How had they come together?

What had they found in the
poor, itinerant Teacher they followed?

Their leader...
This Jesus...
more enigmatic.
Ordinary carpenter.
Extraordinary miracle worker.
Undistinguished Galilean.
Astonishing Teacher.

Little in common.
Oddly compelling.

*

Nicodemus
Prominent Pharisee.
Privileged.
Principled.
Powerful.
Granted access to the inner chambers
of the High Priest.
Granted audience to the marbled halls
of the Roman governor.

"What am I doing here?"
Thought Nicodemus.
Weighing his choices...
step out of the darkness
or
return to the comfort of his hearth.

The part of him that wished to stay
battled with the part of him that wished he had never left home.
The secretive man hidden by the night was...
Captivated.
Curious.
Cautious.

Nicodemus leaned heavily against a boulder.
Feeling the pressure intensely.
One of only a few among the Sanhedrin
willing to consider the teacher's message.
Had watched and listened to Jesus as he…
Moved
easily among the people.
Managed
to cut through hypocrisy.
Maneuvered
around the politics.
Ministered
to the afflicted.

He found himself…
Measuring
the man.
Marveling
at his miracles.
Mesmerized
by his message.

Earlier in the day,
Nicodemus leaned against a column
in the shelter of the Temple porch.
Listened to another lesson.
Stretched his thinking.
Challenged conventional wisdom.
Admired the connection
with those listening with a heart to learn.
Smirked within when he rebuffed the
pious platitudes
of the priests
that even Nicodemus found so…
pompous.

Inquiries
always probing.

Insight
always penetrating.

Inferences
always piercing.

He could no longer sit quietly on the side.
Too many questions swirled in his head.
Too much longing in his heart.

His insatiable need to know
brought Nicodemus to a grove of olive trees.
Just outside the
campfire of a carpenter.
Alone in the shadows.
In the deep of night.

*

A lifetime of inner conflict lasted seconds.
Nicodemus pushed away from the rock hiding his approach.
Furtively glanced down the road
toward the Temple walls high above the valley.
Fearful of being caught in a
compromising conversation
with a man his
colleagues held in contempt.
Began moving slowly and quietly toward the light.

He paused, eyes wide,
when a twig underfoot crackled.
Deafening noise in the silence of night.
The two men seated at the campfire
stopped their soft conversation.
Stared intently into the blackness.
Right at him.

"Now or never,"
Nicodemus thought.

*

Nicodemus stepped into the flickering light.
Pulled the cloak from his face.
The rabbi's disciple,
tense with recognition,
called quickly for the others to wake.

Nicodemus.
Respected ruler in the temple court.
Stood uncomfortably in the firelight,
bent beneath the low branch of an olive tree.

Jesus.
Sat curiously within the warmth of the fire at his feet.
Deep shadows hid his eyes,
but not his smile.
Unassuming.
Unguarded.
Unpretentious.

A brief moment.
Ponderous with anticipation.
Each waited on the other to
make the first move.

Word of greeting.
Welcoming gesture.
Jesus motioned toward a nearby stone,
inviting Nicodemus to share
the warmth of the fire.
The warmth of his hospitality.

Jesus and Nicodemus.
Split a few leftovers from the evening meal.
Chatted about...
everything
and nothing.
until...
A pregnant silence enveloped the camp.

Seeing Nicodemus troubled and anxious,
Jesus stirred the ashes with a sturdy branch.
Gently stoked the dying embers.
Allowed the elder rabbi a chance to gather his thoughts.
Nicodemus started to speak.
Closed his mouth again.
Searching for words.

Jesus looked up from the fire.
Lifted an eyebrow.
Smiled a disarming grin.
"Nicodemus, take a breath.
It's okay.
What brings you to our camp tonight?"

One question changed a life.
An opening through which even
a conflicted Pharisee could walk.

Nicodemus stared at Jesus.
Mind spinning with a thousand questions.
Heart thumping through his chest.
Palms sweating despite the evening chill.
Cleared his throat.
Spoke quietly to this man who
so upset the status quo.

"You are a Teacher who has come from God.
No one could perform the miracles you do
if God were not with him."

Those rehearsed words fell quickly from Nicodemus' lips.
His well-prepared speech faltered.
Voice faded.
Quiet never echoed so loudly.
Broken only by…
popping of the campfire and
nervous tapping of his right foot on the dried grass.
He looked at Jesus,
pleading for help.

Nicodemus heard…
"You cannot enter the kingdom of heaven
unless you are born again."
Felt the eyes of Jesus bore deeply into his soul.

Not at all the response he expected.
"I offered a compliment.
Acknowledged his God-given power.
Got a
riddle in return."

"I don't understand.
No one enters again into his mother's womb."
A feeble attempt at humor to buy a little time.
Jesus chuckled.
"Not what I meant, my friend…
and you know it."

Nicodemus heard…
"Born of the spirit."

The two teachers settled into
deep dialogue.
Well into the night.
Jesus drew Nicodemus into the
debate for all eternity.

If you want to experience the Kingdom of God…
Forget the signs and miracles.
Forget the rituals of religion.
The rote.
The routine.

The Kingdom of God is not…
Passed down by family.
Earned by position.
Given to a nation.

The Kingdom of God requires…
Radical change.
Real commitment.

"How can this be?
You ask too much.
I'm too old to change.
This has been my life…"

"You are Israel's teacher, and still you do not understand?"

Nicodemus heard…
The Kingdom of God is…
Personal.

Nicodemus sat on the boulder,
losing all track of time.
Challenged core beliefs.
Confronted entrenched paradigms about…
His life.
His faith.
His God.

Faced his reluctance to accept
what his heart began to believe.

Nicodemus put up one last defense.
Jesus shook his head.
Held up his hand.
Nicodemus stopped his argument mid-sentence.

Jesus whispered.
Nicodemus heard…
"For God so loved the world,
that he gave his only Son,
that whoever believes in Him should not perish,
but have everlasting life."

The Curious convicted.
The Convicted converted.
The Converted celebrated.

Late into the early morning hours,
long after all the teacher's disciples
wilted with weariness,
Jesus and Nicodemus

embraced in the
dying light
of a campfire...

and the
dawning Light
of a new day.

The Chase for a New Start

Nicodemus came to Jesus in darkness.

Literally.
For it was the dead of night.

Figuratively.
For he was confounded by words that made him think.

Spiritually.
For he had it all wrong.

Over time, he grew...
Content with the outdated covenant as one of God's chosen people.
Placing trust in his family inheritance of
position and power.
Convinced that his profession earned him the
grace of God.
Thought he understood the nature of God's kingdom.
Like so many others,
he didn't get it.

Give the man credit.
He came to Jesus when others among the ruling council did not.
They heard the same message from Jesus.
Saw the same miracles of Jesus.
Refused to listen with an open heart.

Nicodemus opened his heart and his eyes to a new covenant.
Yet, full understanding came later.
After his encounter with Jesus on the hillside,
one can picture Nicodemus.
Sequestered in study.

Poring over Scripture.
Nights spent in private contemplation.
Days spent in whispered conversations
with trusted advisors
about his encounter with Jesus.
"Could He really be...?"

Like any new Christian embracing
God's gift of grace,
Nicodemus had much to learn.
His world had shifted beneath his feet.

In the beginning,
what was personal was also private.
Few knew of his leap of faith.
Nicodemus chose his words carefully
amid the antipathy of the religious leaders.
(John 7:45-52)
Nicodemus offered
conciliatory comments.
Urged careful consideration.
Cast aside by hatred.
Bullied.
Harassed.
A voice too timid.
A voice among too many.

Later still,
(John 19:38-42)
on the saddest day known to Earth,
Nicodemus broke from his private hiding place.
Used his connections with Pilate.
Publically petitioned to take the body of Jesus from the cross.
No longer caring about the reprisals.
No longer silent in his testimony.
No longer ashamed of his trust in his Savior.

Like Nicodemus,
we find a longing in our hearts to
respond to the intriguing words of Jesus.
We struggle to understand the
robust requirement of belief.

We come to Jesus hidden in the shadows.
Hesitant to join him at the campfire.
When our words seem too feeble to flow,
We hear...
"Take a breath.
It's okay.
What brings you here tonight?"

One question creates an
opening through which any
conflicted person can walk.

And, if willing,
we enter into the debate of a lifetime.

The good news of Christ
cannot be argued.
Only experienced.
Not earned by...
Virtue of your parent's faith.
Professional status or prestige.
The church to which you belong.
The country in which you live.

The good news of Christ is...
a gift of grace,
and, it's...

personal.

"YOU must be born again...."
"For WHOEVER believes..."

It's personal.
It's our choice.

"My sacrifice, O God, is a broken spirit;
a broken and contrite heart you, God, will not despise."
Psalm 51:17

THIRSTY NO MORE

The Story of the Woman at the Well
John 4:4-30

Anna heard him enter through the front door.
Winced at the shouted obscenities.
Another drunken afternoon.

He wobbled to the jar standing in the corner.
Eager for a drink of water to
quench his thirst.
Cool his parched throat.

He tipped the tall jar.
Drained the last of the liquid into a small cup.
Less than a mouthful.
He tossed the cup angrily against the wall.
Screamed another string of curses
at the woman with whom he shared his home.

Demanded water.
Damned her existence.
An age of frustration and futility
released in his voice.
A final squawk heard across the neighborhood.
Shoved the heavy vessel in her arms.
Pushed her out the door,
barring it behind her.

The woman stood.
Angry.

Ashamed.
Stared at the heavy wooden door as people gawked.

Alone…
In the dusty street.
In the withering heat.
In her humiliation.

*

No other choice.
Hefted the heavy jar to her shoulder.
Head down.
Made no eye contact.
Walked quickly and quietly
through the
streets of Sychar.

Along the way…
Men turned their backs.
Catcalls.
Contempt.
Condescension.

Women hurriedly huddled.
Furtive glances.
Whispered words.
Spiteful gossip.

Anna bore the indignities with practiced disregard.
Heard it all before.
Nothing new.
Could recite by heart the litany of abuse.

Every failed marriage…
drew her more deeply into the despairing
depths of lost hope.
Pushed her more profoundly into the tormented
fringes of society.
Unwelcomed.

Unaccepted.
Unwanted.

The man with whom she now lived...
Little more than a means to an end.
Food for private favors.
Shelter in exchange for work.
Not the life of which she dreamed as a girl.
Not the life she had chosen.
Rather a life dropped on her by years of ...
Poor choices.
Ponderous circumstances.
Pitiful conditions.

She recalled.
Her first husband.
Her love.
Relationship to God formed the center of their marriage.
Prayerful.
Faithful.
Worshipful.

Her familiarity with Scripture a source of
constant comfort...
until he died.

The hole in her heart ...
a chasm.
The safety of her soul...
a void.
The assurance of her faith...
a darkness.
The path of her life...
an endless, downward spiral.

*

In time, she passed outside the city.
Breathed a sigh of relief for the welcomed solitude.
Walked toward Jacob's well
shadowed in the trees of a nearby oasis.
Green carpet of vegetation in a barren desert.

In reality, she cherished her time at the well.
Out of town.
Away from the discord at home.
Distanced from the haughty eyes on the streets.
Far from the hateful comments and
harsh condemnations of neighbors.

Solitude
offered
solace.

Some distance from the well,
Anna spotted a dozen men walking toward town.
A moment of mutual recognition.
Jew.
Samaritan.
The Jewish men
ceased their conversation.
Quick looks of disdain directed toward the
Samaritan woman.
Eyed each other in silence.
Each crowding the opposite shoulder of the roadway.

She heard them break into laughter
as they walked away.
Directed at her.
Contemptuous of her...
Race.
Religion.
Reality.

She spat at the ground.
No place in her heart for Jewish men.
Any man for that matter.

She crested the small hill.
Followed the path among the stunted trees
to the ancient well.

Anna saw Him.
Sitting in the sand at the base of the well.
Head back.
Eyes shut.
Cool of the stone
contrasting with the heat of the noonday sun.

She looked around the oasis.
Confused.
Cross.

No one ever came to the well at noon.
Looked back at the man.
Noticed His clothes.
Spat again on the ground.
Another Jew.

Anna backed away.
Sat on her haunches.
Out of sight.
Waiting for Him to leave.
No desire to talk with this stranger.
No desire to hear anything he had to say.

His voice carried across the grass to her hiding place.
"I'm waiting for friends to return with food.
May I trouble you for a drink?"

She pushed aside the bough of the date tree.
The man sat still.
Eyes still closed.
Motionless.
Lips curled into a slight smile.

She glanced back toward Sychar.
Saw the men she passed in the distance.

"Wonderful!"
Her thoughts dripped with sarcasm.
"It will be an hour before they return."

The ridicule of the morning,
heat of the day,
left her in no mood for small talk…
certainly not with a Jew.

She twirled around in the sand.
Dropped the vessel heavily in the dirt.
Straightened her small frame to full height.
Challenging.
Confrontational.

"You are Jew.
I am Samaritan.
How dare you ask me for a drink?"

The man pushed His back against the well to stand.
Leveraging Himself with His arms.
The move of a weary man.

"If you knew the gift of God and who I am,
you would be begging me for
living water."

Conundrum.
Cryptic.
Confounding.

She laughed in His face.
Looked at His hands.
Checked for a bucket at His feet.
Caught Him in an act of boastful exaggeration.

"Living water!"
Voiced in derision.
"Are you greater than Jacob?
He gave us this well for our use.

Through the generations.
Besides…
How can you provide any water?
The well is deep.
You have nothing to use to bring it up."

The Man chose not to take her bait.
Leaned back against the well.
Sat on its rough stone wall.
No argument.
A mysterious smile.
Clearly enjoying the conversation.

Twisted His shoulders.
Stared into the depths of the well.
"Drink this and you'll get thirsty in a few hours.
Drink the water I provide.
Never thirst again.
Ever."

She stared at Him.
Unsettled by His confident
demeanor.
Uneasy with the direction of the
dialogue.
Her stomach fluttered.
Voice caught in her throat.

Years of loneliness and isolation left her…
Victimized.
Vulnerable.
Vanquished.

The time it took for Him to speak left her…
Curious.
Open.
Listening.

All the water she needed…
for the rest of her life…

Never again to face
hostile neighbors.
Never again to
walk alone to a distant well.
Never again to
suffer ridicule.

For the first time in memory, she
allowed herself to dream.
"If only such water existed..."

Anna breathed a heavy sigh.
Entertained a split second of hopefulness.
Could life really be different?
Tears welled in her eyes.
Words little more than a hoarse whisper,
"Where can I find this water?
I don't want to have to draw water like this anymore."

A woman's heart
in a
world of hurt
needed badly to hear a
word of truth.

Her posture begged Him to answer.
Eyes locked in silence.
Each pleading with the other for understanding.
Anna felt a chill in her heart.
His steady gaze cut through her pain to her aching spirit.

He eased Himself back to the sand.
Rested His head against the stone casement of the well.
Closed His eyes again.

"Go. Get your husband.
Come back.
We'll talk more."

The words pounded like a hammer.
Not a husband.
A place to stay.

A meal ticket.
A roof.

Her halting, honest response revealed her shame.
"I... I have no husband."

The man's voice softened at the sound of her contrition.
Eyes reflected compassion.
Understanding smile warmed His face.

"I know."
Reciting a litany of personal disappointments.
Five failed marriages.
Followed by this abusive relationship.

No hint of judgment.
No trace of sarcasm.
The man's insight into her past...
Grew too uncomfortable.
Hit too close to home.

Anna.
Deflected the course of the conversation.
Back to her comfort zone.
"You are obviously a prophet.
Let's talk about worship.
Our mountain or your mountain?"
Pointless debate.

Worship is not limited to location.
It's spirit.
It's truth.

The conversation continued to narrow its focus.
The hearing of familiar scripture,
almost forgotten.
A longing for the Messiah.
An admission of Call.

Mired in the muck of her self-imposed hell, Anna...
Hated her existence.
Hated what she had become.

Hated the loss of her innocence.
Hated the emptiness of her dreams.
Hated herself for closeting her faith
in the bitterness of her heart.

This man.
This Jesus.
Opened her eyes to her failures.
Opened her heart to her possibilities.
Opened her soul to His words.

The weight of her worry fell away.

She laughed as she had not laughed in years.
Her feet lighter than air.
Eyes danced with the light of salvation.

Jubilation.
Joy.
Justification.

She dropped her water jar,
shattering the loneliness it represented in a hundred pieces.
Raced back into the village
Transformed by grace.
A walking,
talking
testimony
of her encounter with the Messiah.

Her own joy
bringing revival to a sleeping village.

The Chase for Personal Revival

I find it interesting.
Nicodemus.
The Woman at the Well.
Both came to Jesus from different starting points.
Walking different paths.

Nicodemus.
A person of worth who needed to
see himself a sinner.
Followed a path of inclusion.
A heart full of questions.

The Woman at the Well.
A sinner who needed to
see herself a person of worth.
Followed a path of exclusion.
A questionable heart.

Both left their encounter with Christ
in the grip of personal revival.

The Woman.
Lost to love.
Mired in misery.
Locked in loneliness.
Spiraled ever deeper in sin.
Separated from the world around her.
Estranged from her God.

See her.
Really see her.
Watch the transformation.
Evolution of personal revival.

Bound by bitterness,
she hears the invitation of Jesus.
Longs for any relief from her burden.

She listens.
Dumbfounded.

Her life splayed out before her in vivid color.
Acknowledged His insight.
Called Him,
"Prophet."

The "Prophet" probed deeper.
She defensively argued the requirements of faith.
Not as one ignorant of its precepts,
but with familiarity and passion.
One who had once experienced worship,
but squandered its benefit.

Deep in conversation,
fell back on a lost element of hope.
"I know the Messiah is coming."
Jesus responded in a
rare personal revelation.

"I, the one speaking to you, I am He."

Bitter skeptic
to ardent missionary.
In one confession of faith.
The woman leaves her jar of water at the well.
Carries a heart overflowing with living water
from the wellspring of life.
Revival flooding her heart and
covering an entire village.

What causes me to turn away from a life of faith?

Poor choices
I made.

Ponderous circumstances
beyond my control.

Pitiful conditions
I attempt to overcome in my own strength.

Every situation in which I find myself
that is not laid at the throne of God leaves…

A chasm.
A void.
A darkness.
A downward spiral I cannot defeat
until and unless I…
Encounter my Savior at the well
in search of living water.
Grab the chance for
personal revival.

Seek and you will find.
Drink and you will be changed…
And your whole village with you.
It is the natural response to a sip of
God's grace.

Jesus sits patiently by the well.
Waits for us to drink.

*"Restore the joy of my salvation and
grant me a willing spirit to sustain me."
Psalm 51:12*

GRATITUDE OF THE HEART
The Story of the Thankful Leper
Luke 17:11-17

Ten men.
Separated from the world by
distance and disease.

Lepers.
Society's scourge.
Unclean.
Unworthy.
Untouchable.

Rumors flew.
The Healer would pass by.
Any day.

They knew the stories.
The man gave…
Sight to the blind.
Health to the infirmed.
New life to the leprous.

Hope,
long-lost.
Rekindled out of desperation.

Ten men whose sole connection with the world
hung by the thin thread of humanity.
Men who needed,

96

at the very least,
someone to look their way…
To acknowledge their existence.

*

Nine gathered around the late afternoon campfire.
Ate a meager meal 30 yards
from the road leading into the village.
Close enough to see.
Far enough to hide
from those who considered them…
Less than whole.

Nathan.
The tenth among them.
Sat a short distance away from the nine.
A Samaritan.
Outcast among outcasts.
Separated by
race and religion.
Tolerated by
common misery.
Bound by
this insidious malady.

The noise was muted at first.
Grew louder.
Voices reverberated off the rocky hillside.
One by one, the men stood.
Listening for the approaching crowd
somewhere below the crest of the hill.
Buzz of conversation
broken at times by gentle laughter.
Travelers accustomed to the
comforts of companionship.
Friendship apparent
in tone and tenor
drove the lepers' sting of isolation
deeper into their souls.

The Ten stood as the Healer drew closer.
One called out.
Echoed immediately by the others.
Pleading.
Piteous.
Persuasive.

"Can you help us?"
"Healer! Mercy! Mercy!"
"Pity, sir!"
"Please!
"Is there anything you can do…"

Nathan cried out with the others.
Fighting against the
helplessness.
Battling with the
hopelessness.
Needing the Healer's release from
a beggar's life.

Jesus.
The Healer.
Stopped when he heard the shouting.
Saw the men standing
among the trees.
Partially hidden by three large boulders.
Moved instinctively toward them.

Thomas,
Always suspect.
Always cautious.
Grabbed Jesus' arm.
Offered a whispered warning,
"Jesus, stop!
They are lepers."

Jesus smiled at Thomas.
The twinkle in his eyes revealing his understanding,
"I know, Thomas."

Jesus walked up the hill toward the Ten.
Followed at a safer distance by his wary disciples.
The lepers backed away as He neared.
Years of societal convention at work.

"It's okay," Jesus said.
"Don't leave."
Smiling, he added,
"You called me.
Remember?"

Jesus greeted each man.
"How long have you been sick?"
"Are your homes nearby?"
"Where is your family?"

"Have mercy upon us, Master. Do you have any food?"
Jesus looked into the man's eyes,
recognizing the genuine need.
"I think we can spare some bread."

He turned to call one of his disciples,
startled to see Andrew by his side,
already digging several loaves of bread from his sack.
Jesus chuckled at Andrew's eagerness.
Passed the bread to the man.

He looked at each of them again.
Shrugged his shoulders.
"We must go."
Jesus and the disciples headed back toward the road.
Took a few steps.
Turned back to the Ten.
"Go and show yourselves to the priests."

With those words,
He playfully clapped a disciple on the back.
Quickened his pace to the nearby village
for an evening of rest.

*

The sun set on the day.
The Ten stretched out on their pallets.
Lost in private thought
of their encounter with the Healer.
Ate the bread they had been given.
Talked about the
curious command of Christ.
"Go show yourselves to the priests."
What did it mean?
Should they go?

Rising the next morning,
the Ten began their long walk to the village of the priests.
For no other reason than
the Healer...
This Jesus...
Approached them when no one else would.
Talked with them as ordinary men and not as men
doomed and damned by disease.
Gave them bread to meet their need.
They walked because this Jesus told them to do so.
Faithful to His command,
they set off to visit the priests.

*

As they went on their way,
the men waded across a stream.
Banks steep on both sides.

Nathan.
Entered the flow.
Slipped on a mossy rock,
falling to his knees in the
clear, slow-moving water.

Nathan sat in the languid shallows of the small stream.
Catching his breath.
Weary already from the journey.

He stared at his reflection in the water.
Sitting as still as the trees that lined its banks.
Eyes opened wide in shock.
The sight beyond comprehension.
Skin...
No longer mottled.
No longer covered in sores.
No longer white with the scourge of leprosy.
Smooth as that of a child.

Slowly pushed back the hood of his robe.
The sun's light revealing his features.
He watched in the water.
Brought his fingers to his face.
Touched lightly his cheeks,
searching for the
sores, scabs, and scars
with which he had lived for so many years.

Gone.
All gone.
He brushed his left ear ravaged by the
insidious disease that had eaten away at his body.
Smooth to his touch.
Stared at the back of his hands.
Once gnarled and useless.
Now youthful and strong.
Just as he they looked before leprosy made him a
pariah among the people.

Looked again into the stream.
The man in his watery mirror grinned back at him.
Regenerated.
Restored.
Renewed.

Such overwhelming joy
lifted Nathan's soul!
Jumped.
Danced.

Splashed and frolicked
like the child he once was.
Plunged himself into the stream with a shout of exultation.
Rising out of the water.
Laughing in delight.

The Nine looked down on him from the opposite bank.
Stunned expressions.
Convinced of his madness.

Nathan stared at his companions in amazement.
He could see.
They, too, had been healed.
Arms stretched to the sun,
he spun around like a child at play and shouted,
"I'm clean!
I'm clean!
I'm clean!"
He threw off the soaked cloak that once hid his disease.
Showing them his arms and legs.
"You, too, are clean.
Look at yourselves!
Look!"

The men pulled up the sleeves of their garments,
Inspected their limbs.
They gasped in surprise.
Looked at each other.
First one.
Then another.
Then another.
Joined in the chorus of celebration.
Exuberant!
Exultant!

One lost his balance.
Rolled down the bank into the creek.
Laughing in delight and surprise.
Others jumped in.
Hugging companions.
Hugging Nathan.

The revelry diminished.
Excitement yielded to the enormity of the moment.
They stood in the stream.
Soaked to the marrow.
Stared in amazement.
Their ragged breathing slowly returning to normal.

Nathan.
Whispered as he looked again at his hands.
"That's why he told us to go to the priests.
He healed us.
The priests will let us go home.
Let us worship again.
The priests will declare us clean."

Silence settled into their hearts.
Anticipating what it meant to be clean again.

One by one.
They crawled out of the streambed.
Some ran toward the priests' village.
Some headed home to their families.

Nathan.
Watched them go.
Each in his own direction.
Caught up in their enthusiasm,
he sprinted down the path from which they had come.
Back to Samaria.
Back to his people.
Back home.

Suddenly, he froze in his steps.
Looked again at his hands.
Felt his face again.
With resolve,
set off in a new direction.
Toward the village where they met
the Healer.

*

Nathan entered the town,
stopping the first person he saw.
A young boy about the same age as his son at home.
Breathlessly, he asked,
"Do you know?
Is he still here?
Has Jesus left?"

The boy looked suspiciously at the man in ragged clothes
who was smiling from ear to ear.
"He left.
About an hour ago.
Said they were going to Jerusalem."

Nathan ran through town on the road leading to the Jordan River.
About two hours later,
he rounded a bend in the path.
Saw Jesus and his disciples a short distance ahead.
Sprinted toward Jesus,
shouting to catch his attention.

"Hallelujah to God.
Lord, please wait for me!
Praise to the Lord Almighty!"

Jesus stopped.
Waited as the man neared.
Recognizing him immediately as the quiet one
who yesterday stood at the back of the crowd of lepers.

Nathan.
Bowed in reverence before his Healer.
"How can I thank you for your great gift?
Look at me! I'm healed!
You healed me!
The mercy you granted was more than I could ever expect.
Why would you do such a thing?"

The words and phrases rolled off
his tongue and

from his heart.
Caught between each ragged breath.
Deep with gratitude and meaning.
He looked at Jesus.
"Thank you seems so inadequate.
You are truly a man of God."

Jesus helped him to his feet.
Pulled his water flask from his shoulder.
Gave Nathan a refreshing drink.
The men hugged each other.
Shared a life-changing connection.
One who had for too long experienced no human touch,
found himself drawn into the arms of God.

After a moment,
Jesus' eyebrows raised in concern.
He looked past Nathan and asked,
"Were not all Ten cleansed?
Where are the others?"

Nathan looked down.
Bearing the shame of ingratitude belonging to the others.
He shook his head.
"They went their own way."

Jesus' countenance fell.
He turned quietly to his disciples,
despair and fatigue written on his face.
"No one has returned except this foreigner."
As if to say,
"What does that tell you about our people?"

Letting that sad truth sink into the hearts of His disciples,
Jesus turned back to Nathan.
Lightened the mood.
"Yet," he smiled,
"You have returned.
We will rejoice in that."

They spoke for a moment of
family, friends, and

future plans.
"Go home. You are well.
Your faith has saved you."

A quick exchange of farewells.
Nathan again offered praise to God.
He walked backwards for a long time.
Afraid to take his eyes off Jesus.
Waved one last time before
turning toward home.

The Chase for Genuine Gratitude

Ten men.
All lepers.
Shunned and sent away by…
Condition.
Culture.
Circumstance.

Cast out of their homes.
Separated from their families.
Unable to worship because they were unclean.
This leper's life.
Untenable.
Tenuous.
Tortured.

Our world.
Filled with those who relate to the leper's life.
Lonely.
Isolated.
Discarded.
Disconnected

Scripture tells us,
"While Jesus was on His way…
In the course of a normal day…
As He was doing all the things He needed to do…
Ten lepers called to Him.

Distanced by a dreaded disease.
Ten outcasts of society
begged for mercy."

They shouted for compassion to the man on the road.
Responding not with a shout.
Jesus closed the distance between them.
Spoke quiet words.
To stay safely at a distance…
To shout a command and keep walking…
Fails to fit the
character of Christ.

The story begs the questions:
How often do I hear the hurting voices?
Weigh the inconvenience of setting aside
the plans I made?
How often do I stay on my path?
Content to keep my distance.
Shout pearls of pious platitudes
to those who call to me…
"Go find the priest!"
"God bless you!"
"I'll pray for you!"
"Keep the faith!"

Jesus.
Always a perfect example of ministry.
As I go on my way,
I must hear the cry of the afflicted.
Set aside my plans.
Close the distance between us.
Bring quiet words of encouragement
to those who need to hear them.
Take an active part in their healing.
Such is the nature of ministry.

The lepers teach a lesson in obedience.
Jesus made no grand pronouncement of His
intention to intervene.

Nor did He heal them immediately as He had healed others.
A simple command.
"Go see the priests."
A necessary requirement to be pronounced clean.
A measure of hope buried
within His words.

Healing began with that first step of obedience.

The initial response of the lepers
begs another question:
How often do I rot in my misery?
Wallowing in self-pity?
Waiting for a...
miraculous flash of lightning?
Inexplicable burning bush?
Any sign of His Godly intention?

When I hear the command of Christ,
when I sense His direction,
I must trust.
I must obey.
From that initial step of obedience to His command,
blessings flow.
"As we go" about His business.

The lepers' reactions teach one last thing.
Ten experienced healing.
The Bible tells us so.
Nine went on their way...
Celebrating the gift of physical healing,
indifferent to the One who granted such grace.
Self-indulgence
prevented them from receiving the greater gift...
An eternal relationship with the Healer.

The one leper demonstrated the rarity of
genuine gratitude.
Returned to Jesus.
Fell at His feet.

Thankful.
Worshipful.

This man.
Our Nathan.
Scared for his life.
Scarred by his disease.
Experienced grace beyond physical healing.
Experienced spiritual transformation.
Found new life in Christ.

It begs the final question:
How many blessings have you and I left undiscovered
because we did not return to Jesus in gratitude
as the source of our healing?

Give thanks to the Lord, for He is good;
His mercy endures forever.
Psalms 107:1

TO SEE THINGS CLEARLY
The Story of the Blind Man from Bethsaida
Mark 8:22-26

Eli stood slowly,
smiling gratefully at his two friends
lying around the campfire.
Fingers of flame
flickered in vibrant tints of red and orange.
Distorted by tears of utter joy.

Staring pensively at the Sea of Galilee below,
he closed his eyes.
Shook his head.
As if shaking away a dream
too good to be true.

When he opened his eyes,
the scene before him had not changed.
The bronze haze of the setting sun.
The golden glistening crests of
distant waves on the darkening waters.
Stunning in its ordinary beauty.
Glancing back at his friends, he thought,
"They see this every day.
How can they not marvel at the sight?"

Eli laughed quietly.
Filled with a sense of wonder.
Each step down the rocky hill took him
toward the sea

a mile or so below.
Arms held low to his side.
Fingers extended.
Touched lightly the top of the
waist-high grass in the field.
Green and yellow hues as far as his eyes could see.
Fading into the darkness.
Broken only by the dark gray, volcanic stone
jutting through the turf.
Each tall blade of grass waved in unison
in the whispered breath of the breeze.
His dark eyes,
alight with new life,
followed the wind's path up the hill.

A shore bird glided overhead.
Dark brown markings on its neck and wingtips.
Feathered symmetry.
Perfect patterns.

Turning in a slow circle,
Eli gazed at the sun
as it disappeared behind the hills
rising steeply above the water.
Yellow light muted by a shroud of
translucent, bronze haze.

Eli sank to his knees.
The world laid out clearly before him
for the first time
in more than 20 years.
Tears fell from his healed eyes as he recalled
his encounter with The Healer.

*

Just days before…

Two friends.
Childhood companions.
Led Eli from his village
tucked in the hills of Upper Galilee.
Spurred by rumors that The Healer drew near.
A dirty strip of cloth covered his useless eyes.
Blind since the fever struck as a child.

The three travelers arrived in Bethsaida,
a tiny village on the northeast shore
of the Sea of Galilee.
Waited impatiently for Eli's chance for healing.

The Healer and His disciples walked along the path from
Capernaum into Bethsaida.
Passing through on their way north.
No intent to linger.
There would be no crowds in Bethsaida.
Its people previously rejected the Teacher's
Message and miracles.
Far too jaded.
Far too jaundiced.
Far too skeptical
to embrace new understanding.

Jesus approached the village.
Eli's companions lifted him to his feet.
Called out to The Healer.
Bowed in respectful greeting.
Eli stood still as stone,
listening to the shuffling of men as they approached.
His heart beat faster.
Anxious.
Anticipating.

"Please, sir," they begged.
"We know you can help our friend."

Vouched for his goodness.
Undeserving of his affliction.
Tried every possible cure.
Nothing worked.

"We've seen your power.
Please, sir."

Eli stood quietly.
Embarrassed at their praise.
Overwhelmed by their plea
on his behalf.

Though blind to the world around him,
Eli felt the gaze of The Healer within his soul.
He heard His voice,
quietly praising Eli's companions.
"Greater friends he could not have."

Eli sensed his presence.
Heard the scrape of his foot
as he stepped in front of him.
Felt his breath upon his cheek.
Listened as he whispered,
Lost in whispered conversation.
Probing.
Private.
Personal.

After a moment,
The Healer took him by the elbow.
Led him through the city streets
beyond the northern gate.
Jesus serving as the
eyes of the blind.

They walked together.
Eli's friends followed discreetly.
Out of earshot of the quiet conversation.
Fearful of intruding.

Watching in wonder as both men smiled.
Heard the soft laughter of a friendship forming.
Paused along the way as Jesus
drew Eli close for deeper dialogue.

Some distance from Bethsaida,
Jesus steered Eli from the beaten path.
Near a cluster of boulders.
Sat Eli on one of the stones.

Eli quit listening for a moment as Jesus
gently peeled the bandage away.
Embarrassed as one
victimized by an unsympathetic society.
Vacant eyes stared into nothingness.
Covered in the thin, dried paste of the salve
applied that morning.

The Healer spit into his own hands.
Gathered the moisture on his fingertips.
Wiped away the dried crust of disuse
from Eli's eyes.

Knowing how disorienting new sight could be,
Jesus turned him gently away
from the glare of the sun.
Keeping his strong hands upon his shoulders,
Jesus asked,
"Do you see anything?"

Eli opened his eyes to
a world mottled in color.
Vague images in the distance
moved to and fro...
Indistinguishable.
Indecipherable.

In an almost inaudible voice filled with surprise,
he answered,
"I see people.
They look like trees walking around."

Jesus moved in a second time.
Placed his hands on the man's eyes.

"Now," he asked again.
"Is that any better?"

Eli opened his eyes a second time.
The world lay before him.
Vibrant.
Vivid.
Clearer than the childhood memories
locked in the corners of his mind.

Spun slowly.
Took in the beauty around him
until, at last, he turned
his gaze to The Healer.
Eye to eye.
Face to face.
Smile to smile.
Not just with The Healer,
but with his Savior.

*

Eli looked once more around him.
Thought about the blur of events that
brought such clarity.
Took his eyes from the beauty of the scene below.
Turned to his friends around the glowing campfire.
Closed his eyes.
Opened them.
Unable to contain the grin that spread across his features.
Once blind
to the world around him.
Now he could see.
Once blind
to the One who touched him.
"Now," he said. "I see."

With a shout of praise to God on High,
Eli ran up the hill and embraced his friends.
Laid awake all night
counting the stars.

The Chase for Discernment

Five short verses.
One unnamed blind man.
One wondrous encounter with
The Healer.

On its surface,
little more than another quick miracle
revealing the power of Jesus.
Its significance passed over too quickly
because we have proven ourselves a little too...
Jaded. Jaundiced.
Skeptical.
A little too much
Bethsaida
in all of us.

Find three essential truths
buried between the lines.

First...
a story of
friendship and faith.

Friends.
Sensitive to a greater need.

Friends.
Caring for a lifelong companion
locked in darkness.

Friends.
Faithful enough to seek
The Healer's touch.

116

Friends.
Taking a friend from
physical blindness to
physical sight.
From spiritual blindness to
spiritual insight.

Blessed is the one with faithful friends
willing to lead them to
The Healer.

I wonder...
are we such friends?

Secondly...
a story of Christ's
sensitivity and compassion.

Perhaps
the long walk from Bethsaida
convinced Jesus of the man's
genuineness and goodness...
of his heartfelt trust in Jesus as his best hope
for healing and salvation.

The quiet conversation opened the floodgates of
God's compassion extended
to a hurting soul.
Compassion that still flows to our world today.
Available to all who
sincerely seek it.

Thirdly...
A story of God's
process of salvation.

The account serves as a reminder that
spiritual insight takes time...
that God reveals His will to us...
but only as we need to know it.
A process designed to prevent us from becoming ...
Disoriented.

Dazed.
Disconcerted…
By the breadth and depth of
His plan for our lives.

In the light of our new day,
God extends His grace to
clean our eyes of the
thin salve of self-indulgence
that prevented us from seeing
His will in the first place.

Then…
as we grow accustomed to new understanding,
He touches us again to enable us to
see His will more clearly with…
New eyes.
New clarity.
New outlook.

We bask in the beauty of
life lived in the love
of Christ
and His plan for us.
We turn our gaze to the Son.
Eye to eye.
Face to face.
Smile to Smile.
Not just with our Healer,
but with our Savior.
With a shout of praise to God on High,
we run to embrace the world around us.

"Where can I go from your Spirit?
Where can I flee from your presence?
Even the darkness will not be dark to you;
The night will shine like the day,
for darkness is as light to you."
Psalm 139:7, 12

A TALE OF TWO HEARTS
A Story of Mary's Anointing of Jesus
Matthew 26:6-13

One heart.
Alone against the wall.
In self-imposed isolation.
Embittered.
Estranged.

Cheerless.
Cynical.

His countenance
a picture of misery amid the glad-hearted
fellowship of friends too long apart.
The celebration cascaded around him,
darkening his mood.

Judas Iscariot.
Passionate nationalist.
Keeper of the purse.
Smooth talker.
Smooth thief.
Furrowed his eyebrows.
Anxious.
Annoyed.
Laughter filled the home.
Soured his mood.
Everything was happening too fast.
Spiraling out of his control.

119

Didn't like the way that felt.
Not at all.

So...
He stood alone.
Pouted.

He knew why they were here.
Judas recalled the meeting a year ago.
Just outside the village.
An encounter with Simon.
A leprous Pharisee isolated from his ministry by the loathsome disease.
Judas might have felt compassion for anyone else.
Not for Simon.
Judas hated the Pharisees.
Not some of them.
All of them.
Considered their style of religion irrelevant.
Placating the powerful for
personal profit.

Judas knew Jesus.
Believed in his power.
Knew Jesus would bring healing.
"At least make him pay," argued Judas at the time.
"We could use the money."

To this day,
Jesus' disappointed eyes haunted him.

Judas scanned the room.
Impatient.
Here they were.
Months later.
Gathered in Simon's home.
Like they were all great friends.
Jesus.
Simon.
Lazarus.
Mary and Martha.

120

The Twelve.
Gathered for a meal together.

Judas reviled the revelry.
Heart wasn't in it.
He wore a scowl that
made sure everyone knew it.

James approached.
Two goblets of wine in his hands,
extending one to Judas in an effort to draw him in to the merriment.
His act of kindness stopped cold by a scornful
gaze of contempt.
James veered quickly toward John standing nearby.
Unwilling today to deal with Judas' hostility.

Judas puckered his lips.
Stared at his back as he sidled away.
Screwed up his face and muttered,
"Fools!"

With each passing day,
Judas felt more isolated.
Discontented.
Distanced.
Disconnected
with the Master's message.

Like iron to a magnet.
Judas gravitated naturally to
Jesus and his ministry.
At least in the beginning.

Amazed
at His power.
Astounded
by His preaching.
Awed
by His presence.

He joined the Twelve eagerly and readily.
Visions of change.
Visions of a new Jewish nation
dancing in his
heart and head.

Judas was certain
Jesus was the Messiah.
The one who would drive the Romans into the sea.
Rescuer.
Ruler.
Redeemer.

Judas closed his eyes to think again of his schemes.
Sit beside the king on his throne.
Abounding in riches
beyond avarice.
Abiding in dominion
beyond his ambition.

Judas heard the recent change in tone.
Jesus spoke not of victory,
but of death.
Most definitely different.
Somewhat somber.

Despite the uplifting chatter
around him this day,
Judas felt no joy.
Drawn into the conversations,
Judas plastered a smile on his face that
reached no farther than his lips.
Stood stoically,
sullenly,
among those he called friends,
scheming for a way to get his revolution back on track.

Simon's adoration
of the Master
sickened him.

Lazarus' celebrity status as
"resurrection man"
infuriated him.

The fawning
servitude of the sisters
embarrassed him.

The inability of the other disciples
to see the changes in Jesus
left him…
Disenchanted.
Disillusioned.
Disheartened.

When Simon called them to dinner,
Judas reclined near Jesus.
Determined to vent his growing bitterness.
Remind Jesus of the high stakes
game they were playing.

Judas waited for his moment.
Not tasting a
morsel of his meal.

*

Another heart
Alone against the wall.
Waited for its moment.
Worshipful.
Reverent.

Serious.
Solemn.

Mary fumbled with the basket of bread.
One eye on her labor.
The other on her Lord.

123

She listened to men
glad-hearted in raucous conversation.
Shouting boisterously to be heard above the
laughter echoing through the house.
Content in each other's company.
Fellowship of friends.

Mary left her sister near the fire.
Pulled an alabaster jar from inside her tunic.
Draped it carefully around her neck.
Picked up a nearby towel.
Slid quietly around the table.
Back against the wall.
Inconspicuous.
Unobtrusive.
Ignored.

Jesus reclined on the couch in front of her.
Feet extended near her place along the wall.
She stood behind him,
gathering her courage.
Mary closed her eyes.
Took a deep, calming breath.
Crouched behind the couch where he reclined,
kneeling at her Master's feet.

*

Satisfied and content with
food and fellowship,
Jesus caught unusual movement in the corner of his eye.
Glanced behind Him.
Intrigued to see Mary kneeling.
Head bowed.
She prayed softly.
Indistinguishable words addressed to His Father.
Small hands
clasped a tiny alabaster jar
dangling from her neck.
Spellbound.

Silently.
Jesus watched.

*

Mary knew his eye was on her.
Self-conscious.
Ill at ease.
Tears welling in her eyes.

With a swift and a practiced motion,
Mary broke the delicate top from the alabaster vial.
Room filling instantly with the
sweet aroma of nard.
Lavish.
Luxurious.
Lingering.

Conversation ceased.
Curious.
Concerned.
Every eye turned her way,
drawn by the scent.
Once unnoticed,
now the center of rapt attention.

With deliberate effort,
Mary dribbled the perfume on Jesus' feet.
Evenly applied the liquid with her long, black hair.
Taking her time.
Humming a solemn song of mourning.
Dried His feet
tenderly with the towel
draped around her shoulder.

*

Judas.
Rose to his feet in shock.
Outraged at the break in propriety.

125

Hardly her place.
Hardly the time.
Excessive.
Extravagant.
Others in the room grumbled.

*

Ignoring the murmurs of discontent,
Mary crawled forward on her knees.
Peter, sitting to Jesus' right,
backed away to give her room.
Too stunned to speak.
Too shaken to protest.
The wooden couch squeaked along the rocky floor
as he pushed it aside.

Mary raised her head.
Haunting song still softly on her lips.
Reverent.
Prayerful.
Staring for a moment into the marveling eyes of her Lord.
Took the small ampule of expensive liquid
in trembling hands.
Poured the last of the nard
anointing Jesus' head.
Drying again the excess with her towel.

Mary sat back on her heels.
Stared into the face of Jesus as tears fell freely.
An eternity of unspoken words between them.
Mary sensed the significance of the moment.
Jesus knew.

Mary felt her master rest
his hand on her head.
He smiled in gratitude, fighting to hold back tears…
His heart.
Her heart.

Savior.
Child of God.

*

One heart.
Stood speechless.
Quickly scanned the room.
Expected someone to speak against the gesture.
Wasteful.
Worthless.

The cost of the perfume registered in his
greed-riddled mind.
"If sold at market, that perfume would bring..."
He could feel the weight of the coins in his purse as if it had been...
His to sell.
His to pocket.
His to invest.

Unrestrained fury.
Angry at Mary.
Angry at Jesus.
Angry at the world.

"Jesus!
Why did you allow this waste?
This perfume could have been sold for a high price."
Quickly covering his greed,
Judas sighed deeply.
Clucked his tongue.
"We could have given all of this to the poor."

*

Mary blushed.
Backed away.
Tried to blend into the background.
Mortified.
Humiliated.
Embarrassed.

Jesus clasped her hand.
"Don't go," he whispered.

Sitting up on the couch,
Jesus rubbed his face with her towel.
Dried the perfume still running down his cheek.
Rubbed his eyes.
Took a moment.
Let his frustration fade.

"Why are you bothering her?"
Looked first at Judas,
then the others.
Confident He commanded their complete attention.

"She has done a beautiful thing for me."
Jesus gazed at Mary,
face hidden in her hands.
"She anointed me for burial.
I tell you," Jesus said as led her from the room,
"she will be remembered for her actions this day."

"But, she…"
Judas began to protest.
Jesus whipped his head around.
The flash of his eyes freezing
the words on his tongue.

Judas glanced around the room,
hoping for support to press his point.
He saw…
Sheepish embarrassment.
Averted eyes.
Telling him all he needed to know.

*

Mary leaned against the shoulder of her Lord.
Felt the strength in his arm.
Heard the whispered words
of understanding.

She was…
Disquieted
by the full understanding of what

the coming days would bring.
Sensitive
to the point of clarity.

The One who raised her brother from the grip of death
faced the same mortal enemy.
Understood His true nature.
What He was sent to do.

Unconventional act.
Unconditional love.

One heart understood.
She offered its best for him
before
Jesus could offer himself for her.

*

Judas pushed his couch aside,
reeling with rage.
Muttered under his breath to no one in particular.
Stormed through the door
into the darkening dusk.

Walked a distance without
definite destination.
Halted in the middle of the road.
Surprised that he stood atop the crest
of the
Mount of Olives.
Jerusalem's Temple
silhouetted by the setting sun
across the Kidron Valley.

One heart.
More isolated than ever.
Made up its mind.
Disciple.
Defector.

Deserter.
Walked briskly…
Toward the Temple
Toward treachery.
Toward his thirty pieces of silver.

The Chase for Mary's Heart

Two hearts.
Two eternal decisions.

A Judas heart
Attuned only to itself.

A Judas heart walks with Christ every day,
kneading the words it hears
into a formless clump of ugly self-interest.
The clay becoming the potter.
A vain attempt to…

Shape Christ into its creation.
Dictate its will.
Force His hand to act its way.

An approach that leaves a Judas heart
clutching its 30 pieces of silver.
A petty price
for perfidy.

A Judas heart misses the point entirely.
It's not about me.

*

A Mary heart.
Attuned to the life of Jesus.

A Mary heart walks with Christ every day,
molding the message it hears
into a masterpiece of a sacrificial life of service.
Allowing the potter to do His work.

130

Among the sisters of Lazarus,
Mary was the sensitive one.
Mesmerized always by the...
Presence of the Master.
Power of His words.
Passion of His heart.

Perceptive eyes allowed her to see in Jesus
what his closest disciples often failed see.

Our hearts should beat as Mary's.
Gird up our courage
to kneel at His feet.
Act in complete adoration.
Anoint Him with the best we have.

Anoint His feet because we are His servants.
Anoint His head because we are keenly aware of
salvation's sacrifice.

Mary's heart is love.
Extravagant.
Excessive.
Extreme.
Love that breaks the top off of that part of us
selfishly set aside for ourselves.
Pours it out in recognition of His sacrifice.
His love...

"All to Jesus I surrender."

Mary demonstrated in the outpouring of her adoration of Christ that
love is humble.
Seeks to serve unnoticed,
yet without reservation.
Holds nothing back in fear of what others might think.
Gives all because...

"All to Him I owe."

A Mary heart kneels at the feet of Christ,
accepting His life-changing grace...

"Sin had left a sinful stain,
He washed it white as snow."

"Whom have I in heaven but you?
And beside you, I desire nothing on earth.
My flesh and my heart may fail, but God is the
strength of my heart and
my portion forever."
Psalm 73:25-26

AFTERTHOUGHT

I've chased after a great many things in my life.
Some good.
Some not so good.

Though they may be different,
reflecting the culture of my century,
the litany of mistakes I've made in my Christian walk
put me on par with
Zacchaeus.
Nicodemus.
The Woman at the Well.

The times of assurance and trust
not all that different from
Mary.
The Blind Man from Bethsaida.

Therefore,
the question is a good one.
What am I chasing?
What are you chasing?

I think back to my time with my grandson.
"Chase me, Grandpa!"
The delight I experience in the chase.
I can't help but smile
when I think of the joy on his face
when I catch him.

Surely God feels even greater joy when we
chase and capture
His heart.

Surely, it delights Him so much that He can't wait to say,
"Chase me again, Child."
He knows we learn so much about who He is by...
Pursuing His will.
Chasing that life worth living.

Thanks to God!
It is a merry chase!

ABOUT THE AUTHOR

D r. Kirk Lewis began a new ministry in 2013 by publishing his first book *Put Away Childish Things* with Xulon Press. *Put Away Childish Things* won a Christian Writers Award in 2014 and has drawn positive reviews for its message and imaginative writing. He continues to periodically publish devotional thoughts in a blog called "The Searcher."

Lewis teaches an adult Sunday School class and is an ordained deacon at South Main Baptist Church in Pasadena, Texas. As a student at Texas Tech University, he served as a Youth Minister at First Baptist Church in Wolfforth, Texas. After graduation, he attended Southwestern Baptist Theological Seminary in Fort Worth, Texas, to pursue a degree in religious education.

Lewis earned his bachelor's degree in 1976 from Texas Tech in advertising/public relations. He earned a master's degree in Education Futures from the University of Houston in 1983 and a doctorate degree in Educational Leadership from Lamar University in 2008.

He worked in public relations in the corporate world before joining Pasadena Independent School District in 1986, leading the district's Communications Department and winning numerous writing awards. In 2000, Lewis was named Deputy Superintendent for Administration in the Pasadena Independent School District before becoming its superintendent in 2006.

Kirk and Robin's family include two sons, Adam and Andrew, who are both married with children. Adam and his wife, Jordan, have two children named Eli and Josiah. Andrew and Melissa were married in 2013 and have one daughter, Lena. All are active members of South Main Baptist Church.

Find out more about the author and his writing by visiting his website at www.drkirklewis.com.

CPSIA information can be obtained
at www.ICGtesting.com
Printed in the USA
LVOW04*0045181115
463078LV00006B/45/P

9 781498 437509